Catchy-Feel-Goods
Part Two

By Danielle A. Deckard

authorHOUSE®

AuthorHouse™
1663 Liberty Drive
Bloomington, IN 47403
www.authorhouse.com
Phone: 1-800-839-8640

First published by AuthorHouse 07/25/2011

ISBN: 978-1-4520-1606-1 (sc)
ISBN: 978-1-4520-1607-8 (hc)
ISBN: 978-1-4520-1608-5 (ebk)

Library of Congress Control Number: 2011910610

Printed in the United States of America

Any people depicted in stock imagery provided by Thinkstock are models, and such images are being used for illustrative purposes only. Certain stock imagery © Thinkstock.

This book is printed on acid-free paper.

A Southern Hospitality Note

If you are just getting here, let me first say welcome; you are accepted here and never separated. Now, please wait while the Lord helps you entertain your next breath; it is all underway. Once again, I am here for more than your daily amusements; driven to give you a real sense of how strong you are, how far you can go, and how far you've come. Dedicating yourself to positive satisfaction will keep you content in life and allow you to prevail throughout every pit of despair. This book is my dedication to where I was and where I am now; you, too, can follow your own lead and make it, just like I have. Come inside and see your true colors by revealing yourself to the aspects of words gone right.

Welcome to my show!

Contents

Dedication

I dedicate this book to everyone, literally! Young and wise, I want you all to pay attention to the "whole" mania. My hope is to allow you to empower your mind and keep it open, so you won't miss out on your miracles! I can prove it to you in *this* book, it's a sure possibility! Get addicted to yourself and rely on more than these words, but the right way, His way! I love you, Jesus, Mom, Dad, Tiffany, Brandon, D2, Jay, and Andre ... *the perfect people you all are.*

Double-Check It Twice

Walk, don't run!

Please don't miss your opportunity; don't let it come and go.
Please don't miss your opportunity; don't let it come and go.
Time moves on and never looks back.
Please don't miss your opportunity; don't let it come and go.

Gotta call Jay and see what he needed.
Pay my cell phone bill, check my accounts.
Take these shoes over to Tiff's for D2.
Prep for this book signing on Friday.
Nails and eyebrows done at 2:00.
And what else?
Where are my keys?

What are you thinking?
What can you tell me about what you see?
Would you like to go there?
Dreams, want them to work?
What is your plan?
Plan on talking to whom to get there?
Prayer and abiding faith will lead you.
Just because great isn't here doesn't mean good can't make it last.
My goodness, your future awaits you!

Please don't miss your opportunity; don't let it come and go.
Please don't miss your opportunity; don't let it come and go.
Time moves on and never looks back.
Please don't miss your opportunity; don't let it come and go.

I have to stop by Mom and Dad's tonight.
Drop off these articles to Dre' for DR!P *Magazine.*
Make it back home to meet with Brandon
and Larry after their 7:00 game.
Then I have to pick up my clothes from the cleaners.
I have to get some rest tonight for sure, because I am
dragging, and I have to wake up early tomorrow!
Where is the nearest sabbatical?
I need one!

A Reflection of Book One-
All I Need Is You

Remember me from "Catchy-Feel-Goods"?

And all that extra, open space on several of the pages?

I made you reflect, reach out, and relate.

And "Completion,"

"Just Me."

So supernatural that magic became your seventh sense.

"Writing was stored within my DNA,"

that's why I gave you *me*,

tenderness in every word.

I'm the reason for this written-in-the-sky production.

Always the lady; first, that is.

All over again.

Expressing My Gratefulness

Jesus, thank you for the "positive push" and
your many blessings. I NEED YOU!
Mom and Dad, you truly locked in the meaning of
appreciation in my life. Thanks for the keys of love.
Tiffany and Brandon, I just love you both, you
always keep me standing tall and entertained.
Jay, you're the definition of a true friend to me;
you've helped me more than you know.
Andre, you accept nothing less than incredible. I'm so relieved
to have you in my life as my friend, mentor, and business
partner. We are taking over the writing industry!
My family on both sides, the Deckard's and the Desautel's, regardless
of how far you are, you have made an impact that is monumental!
Auntie Ethel, you are a prayer queen, you always kept the faith
going in our household, Jesus helped you, and you helped US!
Carney Mosley, you are the king of ideas, calamity, and
creativity! Thank you so much for making sure that I was being
creative every day, while we were out in the rock box of Iraq.
Player with a Passport, coming to a bookstore near no one!
For everyone else, I have come face to face with
your prayers. Thank you for taking the time out to
support me. You are grand and triumphed!
To the Jesus Freaks, I love you! Tell someone your story, too!
I want to sing thank you to all and hold on to
whatever you find that is GREAT!
Lala

Introduction

I welcome the dedicated.

For this book is a dedication to you and me,

to the ones living their purpose.

Those who are consistent without restraints.

Those that thrive off of joy!

The ones that do not need recognition to

realize that they are victorious.

People who still pray for the haters.

Individuals who live holy on the gospel tip of life.

People who make friends just to help another.

Trials that make us stronger.

Hardships prevailing to the flight of our thoughts, leaving everlasting
impressions that dig deeper than any acceptance could ever measure.

Those who let go and let God!

Amen.

Part 1:
Short but Sweet

I Miss You as if I Have Never Seen You Before

I think of you as if you are my brain, while my body belongs to you.

I yearn to smell you daily.

I tend to daydream of how AWESOME you will be in person.

If I were a song, you would be my chorus.

Walking, working, living, breathing, listening, feeling,

seeing, and so much more, includes the images of YOU.

I would never want to get rid of you.

Knowing that I will see you soon, someday, makes me want to

RUSH the day and speed up the night to get to you faster.

You are as tall as heaven and as perfect as they come.

From the moment I heard about you, my soul hasn't

stopped begging my heart to invite you in.

You are my newfound addiction.

Love, let's toast it up!

Cheers.

I want you to find love, peace, passion, and joy, even if it is not spent discovering around or with me.

Never allow yourself to be defined by someone
else, except the one that matters, Jesus.

If you have not been willing to give your life for someone else, then you have never been in love.

Heartbreak is shockingly awful, but falling in love is as sexy as heaven!

Sincerely interested in you!
Realize that I am refreshingly original,
and all that you do keeps me near.

I decided to go skydiving shortly after you abandoned ship!

Honestly, if my heart stops beating it will not hurt as much; then again, neither will breathing in outer space!

Adapting to you has changed my life!

Wouldn't you say?

Won't you please stay?

Actions are more than a gesture used to get
the attention of a beating heart.

Make your life taste good to YOU! Yum!

Your words are much sweeter than any
Lamborghini any day! (Sean G.)

From 2000 and forever, this is what I promise
you, I will not live without you.
Your love is not like money, because it does not come and go.
Permanently you match up with the gasps of air I take.
Still, being next to you is too far for me.

Shine like a light bill only if you can afford to!

Keep your soul pure, for the life in it exceeds
the value of any diamond or pearl.

Under any given circumstance,
own justice within your backbone and heart.

I believe it is very elegant when a person is just HONEST.

After all the bitter and crazy aspects, I believe there is still life to live.

Jealousy is alive, but one should never allow
it to come across their path.

Your personality possesses a burnish that thrills the life of the blind!

My compass is broken.
Therefore, I've lost direction, lost my way.
I'm in autopilot.
I need the needle in my compass back.
I think it may be YOU.

Ever been in a place that keeps you looking haggard?
Whenever you walk inside this place, everything is in a tizzy.
You know this is not the idyllic life, so why go back?
Keep going, for the exit is your escape route to sufficiency.

Learn to be the leading person IN your life.

Be brilliant on your own!

Love it when YOU shine.

No matter what you cannot figure out in
life, you are STILL phenomenal.

So make sure you feel phenomenally!

Soon you will understand.

Gumption!

Make sure that you stroke IT into your ego.

Kick butt and forget about taking names!

Living like others will only stop you sooner or faster.

For some strange reason, people in America think they know poverty.
Think again!

One game you can manage to play alone
and still never lose, tic-tac-toe!

Victorious is the trace of my walk.
Come experience it!

When you possess that motherly characteristic,
you have casualness and nice ideas.

I am the force that risked its life to shut out all.
Thank you, thank you.

You are too kind; the things that you say are so vivid with variations and possess a sensational aroma! Hello, morning.

Life is like popcorn, you never know how it will pop!

Do not create what you have not already earned, for a simple gesture can cause you one less breath of an opportunity.

I would have you any day of the week, poor or rich.

I only respond to what I receive, and that is your motivating spirit.

You only deserve the finest jewels that are discovered from the hidden parts of the world.

Never hide how you really feel, regardless of
the area or situation; SHOW YOU!

Hope it makes you breathe so easily that your lungs crack smiles!

Smile today, for God could not imagine you any other way!

Build your life with your heart.

Secondary, your minds, but include the soul.

Roll your mind in positive directions.

More and more should be what you naturally give.

Less is only best when it comes to pain.

Life is simple; it is YOUR plan that makes it difficult.

Living is happiness.

Be stronger!

Wait for it.
Wait for it.
Your blessing, that is!

Shortly after seeing you, I thought, "Wow, that is some brilliant, handsome creativity right there, but it is quite esoteric."

You have me glowing like a schoolchild.

I just want you to make your move, because I need you!

Whatever is needed, I possess.

Get to know me.

Come show me!

The mirror has taught me that I am bigger than what I see.
It is called inner peace which turns my life on.
What I see is just a subliminal blur of who God sought out
to create, so I could establish a human persona; but what I
possess on the inside is as pure and divine as a newborn.
I walk with more than some artificial, breathless charm
called pride; I walk with strength from Him.

Take a Shot Now

Ever wish you could get things that are of your worth?
I admit that people do things that we would never
realize, unless it was done back to us.
Holding back gets you nowhere.
Ever had the desire to be held and touched by
more than a hand? How about with love?
The world is very cold; you are here to warm it
up with your nonstop pleasures of peace.
Your behavior cannot vouch for your overall consumption
of grief; it only benefits off of what you allow it to do.
Nobody loves me.
Not true.

Does time heal wounds?
Alternatively, does it simply dim the appearance and feel
of things that were touched once upon a time?

Living in the grey area,

Houston, Texas, born and raised.

Purchased for a price that no man could ever afford;

for that, she has worth.

There is not enough money in the world to repay.

It took one unique man to win her heart and award her soul.

There is no other man; there is only God.

Honest interpretation, this is no moment of silence!
Definitely NOT my fashion.
Hurting you is definitely not something I want to
show you; it's not where I'm trying to take you.
Only into pleasing YOU.

I am trying to get richer, but the opportunity of a lifetime only comes when you build it on faith and reality, plus family!

Do not look for anything in your life to go
multiplatinum; make it go DIAMOND!

Code, everybody needs one.

What is yours?

I do not see it like that, because I am not flashy; I am a tropical breeze of hope that shows direction, and everyone wants a piece and feel.

I love HEARING you smile.

Let me ask you this penetrating question:
tell me what you do not expect?
(LePriest Goss & Helen Johnson)

After he broke up with my heart and divorced
my soul, I decided to go skydiving!

Nothing dangerous about time, unless you are wasting it away.

Finding yourself makes everything work out.
Cheers.

DNA of a forever soul = exotic, gorgeous, eccentric, and intellectual

Prayer works when it is defined by honesty!

I pray that you are so blessed that everything in your life feels as if it were painted in "glamour."

Sounds like a love song,
and I could never let anyone turn you down.

I do not just subsist with you; I trust you.

Pretending to be heroic;
litigious is not a trait my character will ever live up to.

Life can be epic.
Constant is death.
Severe cases of sin.
That's right; go with Christ!
(Rewritten for you Mom)

Tell me who has the best experience with being wrong?
Elders,
they can take everything and tell us the future we'll never know.
But they cannot take yesterday.

Part 2:
Raconteur, Version 2

Let Freedom Reign! It is Time to Awake!

America the beautiful. Why are we so forgiving? Are the good deeds in the name of vain? Must I pay for my freedom? Do I have to give up something to collect my freedom? Must I choose a side? Yes to being a democrat? Yes to being a republican? Which one? Why not go with WHO is about RIGHT and NOT WRONG! Did you not get the memo? The president is considered HUMAN and not suspect of a scientific genius who has inevitable stage presence of sheer features! America has fallen beyond the floor; it's seeping through the cracks of the earth and escaping to hells entranceway. Shall we let freedom reign? Down pour, your morals all over what we have been through and are still going through. Relating to war as the dedicated should be charged to an American Express while its Visa has Discovered it! What a suspect the USA has become since the gap of press conferences and abused results have been everything but A+! Black and white, this is far bigger than your shade so consider this. Being hung, burned, disrespected, enslaved, all poverty, RIP. Can you be the one to speak out on OUR freedom? Foolery is written in the daily news, airing out of mind crimes in Iraq, granting libertine amendments with brain washed announcements. Do you possess the chest of a titan or the one of a gnome in a true community? Deception filled diseases and questions of shackled programmed elite members. Impunity of a confident leader can lead humanity to a dirty dollar sign. The rapture of a tactful second without a label or a passed law would definitely be a Discovery Channel moment of unity. Shenanigans in this world operate like clockwork; it is a constant swarming of a sing along gone wrong. Society is not fine because there is not enough to eat. Say what you want, tell your story, sing your song, write it down, but let it out all over the television and inform the news to play what we need. Just get the message across of acceding free of gains to a better world as your undertaking agreement to agree.

X

You're the X-factor of importance.

I can't help but relate you to the most beautiful season around, fall.

Simply, I have fallen for your heart, fallen for your soul.

Unquestionably, you are amazing.

No metaphors or puns, rightfully you are what saves humanity.

Pluto Love

My heart never wants to rest now.

You're my excuse to fly higher.

When? Right now.

You're love, my lover.

No matter what I do without you, you live within every moment.

I expect to be cold when you aren't nearby.

Riding on the Hudson and chasing seagulls around the Statue of Liberty has no mark of fun that's near your level of perfection.

Thank you for taking care of every moment ever spent in my life.

I think it's time you take a trip, a factual, astounding trip.

The Super Friend

Him.

He words things very well and speaks so unselfishly to His people.

One major thing about Him: He never does things halfway.

You can never get bored of His word.

He showed us a fighter which bettered our lives.

Before we ever opened our eyes to the world, He blessed us!

He has gone here and there, near and far, but has

never taken His unchanging hands off our lives.

All He is, ever was, and ever will be is the truth.

He is the greatest habit to possess.

Those unspeakable times, that's just the God in you.

You can and will have it made when you

walk with Him in all that you do.

He comes with no excuses and only desires committed love from you.

The clock will NEVER STOP, so begin eternity with

accepting yourself as His creation and your creator.

He is our super friend.

Got Him?

Jesus.

Hope is the word for the future of survival,

while we as humans keep our heads up.

The sun is not the only light that brings creations.

It is God that makes it epic!

Take advantage of what started as scratch, for the

amazing reality is that truth was found then.

Become a provider with care and intelligence in your mind.

Hate it or have it; don't envy it!

Be with it or have nothing to do with it.

This person is a mogul, grown, driven, and knowing.

They get their strength from the most potent man alive, Jesus.

They give security and time.

As far as something missing, it is that significant other.

The assurance that you never have to worry about anything

again makes this person meant to be with any sane creature.

Singing songs repeatedly is more like the feeling of their partnership.

Allowed to live and gain life every second of

your life is the purpose of this creature.

This person is what we all want to know.

Bearing change is the gift they bring.

This new information is worth finding out.

You can't add to infinity, but you sure can add to its existence.

Predicting what is first and last is redundant;

just live out this very moment.

This all came when God's hands opened.

Come lose yourself in love; let this creature have you completely.

Take me or not; I finally understand the person God created.

Everything else is pointless if I cannot be myself.

Disguising me with dark attire is not my favorite means of style.

What the next believes or considers is their habit.

Be content with you!

Love that skin you are in.

Let your life be lived like the beginning.

The existence of you is so worthy of the Lord's likings.

2011 and Counting

Allow me to give you something to believe in.
The truth that has been spoken about for so
long and it is not alive. A new year.
new face for president.
Wow, and we all thought the world was doomed
to complicated pandemonium.
The USA is a work in progress.
We as the human race are getting stronger as
long as we search and stick together.
We need to gain power with each other and learn to never quit!
Our limits as a country have been surpassed.
Keep your chin up and your eyes to the heavens.
Destiny is our finish line.
We will never be perfect, so there is no need to add pressure.
No more war!
For every human inside and outside of America
will claim evenhandedness together.
I pray that people can see that things are much
warmer and believable when love is involved.

Even to like an idea is a start.
The world is slowly becoming alive.
Its people must follow.
God is giving us something to believe in!
Do not freeze yourself to the past for the future
will unthaw your hurtful experiences.
The economy failing is a result of greed.
The clouds will never block the shine of the sun.
Stand up with a promising thought of consistency.
The people of the USA will not depart from strong words that have
used over a thousand years, consisting of strength and realization.
Side by side we will breathe in the new and recycle the old.
The world is no longer silent, for all of its needs
are placed on a pedestal of reliance.
The time it took to demolish civilization will
gain by your radiant acts of kindness.
Any requests shall be noted, discussed, and welcomed.
Happiness fills this world when we all stand together
praising the Lord for a new day, a much greater day.
No more madness and the world will soon know this.
Dreams are not easy, but they are plausible.
I promise the song has now been sworn to repetition.
A change will come; a change has come.

Wake Up

Thank you Jesus! How are you doing?
Fantastically fabulous, for I am alive another
day in this outstanding world.
My angel is no longer in disguise.
As I look into the mirror, I begin to compliment my star player, me.
Wisdom gained for tomorrow is now obsolete.
Even though I am not sharing love with a man, my heart
still sings inside of its preserved jar, which is its world.
I am saved, and for that, I scream, "Thank you!"
The sun is my backup light to my own flashing luminosity.
The glass being broken lets me know that
my problems are out in the open.
My shadow even mocks my stance of excellence.
I woke up right side up today.
My world isn't shattered; it is given another opportunity.
It's true; praying is simply conversations full of faith.
No need to look at me; I changed, and I am not a victim.
Good morning.

A Day That the Lord Has Made

"Jesus, the life I am about to face today has already been alive to your existence. You are aware of every weary step I will take, every song I will sing, every angry person that will approach my direction, every detour I will have to make, if I will smile more than I will frown. Lord, I ask that you give me strength to be copasetic with this brand new day, the strength that I need to make it a good day today." Amen.

Random Joy

I pray that you are feeling so pleasant that you just want to
smile at the pencil that is lying so nicely on your desk!
I pray that your thoughts are as positive as a two-
year-old child is during a birthday party!
I pray that your hands feel as soft as a newborn
and are as creative as Picasso is!
I pray that your heart has the smoothest beat to
the outmost compassionate jazz song.
I just pray that your smile is brighter than the stars
that twinkle and glow during the night.

The Perfect Decision

I know I deserve you more.
Let me explain what I am fighting for;
what I am subscribing to.
Who loves you?
Who goes crazy every time you have to leave?
Who shows you how special you are?
Who thanks you for the times?
Who has gone through the strain and the evident?
I do, I have, I will, I may, I can, and I am!
Maybe once you feel the thump of your heart, you will hear my name.
A waste of time, this is not!
Zoom on into joy, which is the most important,
perfect decision of your life.

To Come

I look for the day that brings change;

for the day where the sun is no longer surrounded by rain.

When people smile twenty-four hours of the day,

while blessings are being made into friends, and

laughter is heard a mile away.

Pain is against the law to say and feel.

Time is never rushed or constantly watched

when being still lacks acceptance.

Easy enough to say I enjoy work.

Pain-free,

suffering is considered foreign to the world.

Every day is unerringly admirable.

Inkling

We were each other's favorites.

In my heart, we would always be together.

Craziness hit us so much that we grew stronger in one another's souls.

But somehow things changed and making up was not an option.

Stop this fight!

Do you love me?

What happened?

Who is to blame?

Us!

Who knew that all the times we kissed, I was

actually kissing you for the last time.

Your eyes were so pure to me, but they soon became

glass and revealed nothing but a lie!

You blinded me!

Never did I hear why you acted this way with me.

You are not perfect; your motives are no longer unseen.

You will feel what I feel!

Slowly you were revealed, but swiftly you will leave.

I've Already Won

It is faith that makes me stronger.

It is my daily beliefs that will get me there.

I know that rushing is not as smooth as falling in love or flying.

When things happen, that is just the exact.

My back may be at a slant, but the wall is my protector.

I see me breaking down, but I will freeze this very moment.

I will throw it away, for I know the God in me will bring me back.

My all is always given.

Feeling like life is one big dare, yet reality sets

in and allows me to take in the truth.

I have already won regardless of my surroundings!

I can't see how it will work out, but I know it will.

Whatever, I have done, the grace of God has already forgiven me.

Amazingly my problems get easier.

No one else seems to provide help.

Prayer, will you work?

Every day we pray to make it through this day.

We always do.

My life, I will make the best out of you.

Every moment is a blessing and there is so much to look forward to.

We won!

Awareness

I have to see you again.
I want to see you whenever I would like to.
Do not frown.
Only smile; God's grace is shining on your soul right now.
Dance over all that negativity that people try to throw your way.
You are doing well in life, can you not tell?
Keep the Lord first, and you will grow just fine into that
gorgeous, caramelized, sweet-smelling skin of yours.

Fatality of an Overdose

All that know me knew I was addicted to you.
They knew I lived to love your love.
My heart drifted as fast as the dust you swept up when you left me.
My vitals became immune to your life.
Forced to strap me down because of my threatening heart attack,
no one knew you were the cause of this.
I was you; you became me.
Sirens are the music to the people, and "Can you hear?" "Stay with
me," the question asked to me while trying to recover my heartbeat.
Rushing to the hospital, running through
lights, trying to survive through this!
Blood tests say no drugs involved.
People, it's him who's to blame!
He lives deep down inside of me!
This must be my "See you later."
For you I would have died with joy; instead,
I am dying a lonely death.
My priority you became.
I loved your feeling, this feeling!
I have lost it!
One more hit of you would have caused me to go over the edge.
Finally, we know why she has overdosed!
"Why didn't she have what she needed the most?" was the
medic's last statement before I was pronounced near to death.
Look what love has done to me!
I have never been this hurt!
Broken, shaken, and hot!
No way would I make it through this last ride.
I abused you, and I did this to myself!
I overdosed on this man!
Without him, I knew I was dead.

Woman in Rain

Get dressed?

Why should I attempt to get out of bed?

Better yet, why open my eyes when he is not around anymore?

Nothing but thunderstorms hit my heart's every beat.

I can't feel the air any longer.

Every sound disturbs my ears.

My light, will you ever return?

This is not my calling, for I know God has love in store for me!

Does death hurt this bad because heartache

feels like a near-death experience?

No one has even called!

This is no break; you are gone.

Reappear and save my life.

Twenty-two days and twenty-two nights;

if this were an ocean, there would be no life vest available to me.

My skin is so thin without you being its extra layer of warmth.

Please come take me out this storm!

Release me from pain and capture my soul that has become lost.

Raindrops are filling up my life; drown or live,

for I have become the woman of rain.

It is starting to rain again in my life.

Even the sun rains!

I don't know much about sorrow, but I do

know that this is not joy or fun.

Tears are rolling down my face which fluctuated from my heart.

Please don't look my way, for you may catch the feeling of doubt.

Negativity strolls through my veins, as if it were my own blood.

Always Be True

Sometimes it is good to just listen.

You show up at the door, no smile, no stare, only

hidden statements behind your eyes.

She looks down with a look of despair, a look of unwanted feelings.

She must have read something in my words; she

must have heard something in my thoughts.

No, she has felt a cold breeze in the mid-

night calm surrounded by palm trees.

I have no words to say, for I might offend, or

does she seem scared? Scared of me?

Cold and warmth hide behind those sensational eyes,

but why you are so caught up in yourself?

Everything is just not about you. How does she feel?

What happened to her, and what was said?

That is what matters. She matters.

It does not matter what you like or do not like, only

that she feels comfortable, safe, and secure.

It does not matter what you feel like doing or not doing; just allow

yourself to show to her that whatever she wants to do or not do,

that is what you do; even if it is just to go back to

your resting place alone and speak in silence.

Speaking and believing that her day will go

better than it was the day you saw her.

Who Am I to Say?

When I arrive, let the horns play in their highest key.

Make this moment soulful.

It's not a regular day, so allow all the nonchalant to stop

being a menace, and let me tell you who they are.

What justifies this moment will supply your life with

as much nourishment as you will ever need.

Better your sight!

Live your life!

Be alive to your life.

Can you not tell that I came from class, high?

Don't mock another's life; just learn what you

need to finish up so yours can get started.

Who knows you more than yourself?

Don't complain about those moments that aren't

fresh; you cannot control everything.

Let it go!

No need to check into rehab for this; they are closed forever!

Just be careful what you wish for … you just might get it!

Now is your time to stand up with support from the inner self.

Thank you for having me today.

Unforeseen

Excuse me, sir.
In my head, I am viewing one of the wildest
types of handsome I have ever seen.
"Wow," said my eyes, as my palms reach out to touch him.
Although, we are strangers, and I cannot
approach him as if he is mine.
I have to sit and build up my gut.
"Let us go," is what I hear from both sides of me.
Wait!
Relax!
I do not want to run into the middle of this instant crush.
How do I feel about this?
I wore this cat woman style dress with 8 inch heels just to feel
extra sexy so I could make my night exclusively magical.
I am strong, but the strength I feel from this stranger is taking my
breath right out of my lungs, filling it with his sweet massive gasps.
What if I wave my hand in the air to get his attention and then wink?
Will my life ever be the same after this enchanting encountering?
Mate or soul mate?
Let's make our way over to him.
Deep breaths, here I come.
How surprising, he greets me with a handshake
and a warm, "Hello, how are you tonight?"
He has now dressed the atmosphere with sunlight.
Although I know this man is not perfect, he's definitely no mistake.
No super hero, but he is manly.
Body language spoke more than my mouth.
He sure does play fair in the field, I thought.
Standing there in front of him, I had deaf ears
that only involved the beat of his heart.
I know I do not know this man, but he
elevates me with just his presence.
This meeting must figure out why this is happening.
He gently reaches for my hand and says, "Let's
go and understand one another."

You Weren't Looking for This, but It Arrived

Tell me about yourself.

Will you tell me what you have been through?

Give me permission to satisfy your life.

I promise to start directly from my own heart

and then educate you, soaring into yours.

This is real; let me show you why.

First, believe in what I am trying to allow us to do.

Stop me any time you want.

Fall in love, try it; you have it!

The only passing score is a smile.

You are in my life every day, and I want

you involved in everything I do.

Let me replace your doubts with beautiful

restoration and return you to the light.

Restore years and never allow your time to be lost.

No need to watch out for the pinchbeck; the broken heart is over.

I am showing you attention, the best of the best.

No luck here, just blessings between two people.

Can you trust me, love?

High Heels

Heavenly and sexy is how I feel with you on.

Intelligent is the look I go for when I wear you.

Gorgeous is what they call us when we walk past.

High is the level of confidence we have.

Hope is what we give them when they see us.

Elegance is in our strut when we sway.

Exclusive is how I choose you.

Luxurious comfort is your fit, and style is your goal.

Surely flashy, yet just right for my feet.

Little Black Dress vs. Little Black Book

You fit me just right. It seems to bear my game.

No matter your length, you're major, you always fit in any pocket.

Women must own one. Men must use them.

Style is usually fitting. Model is definitely current.

One prized outfit in my closet. Matches with everything I own.

A must to show you off in public;

yet, never to reveal her personals.

A major move is being made when I put you on.

Gathering information usually taking the place of the most current.

A very relaxed yet seductive look you give me. Having

you says I am competent in what you do for me.

You are the truth. You manage my truths.

We create situations. Gossip seeps in and out of you.

Attention-greeter. Attention-seeker.

Did you catch it?

What I'm Hungry For!

Why must I wait?

Why must I believe?

When there is an action to be taken!

A mountain to be conquered and time that is nonstop.

Moves must be made or else I will lose out forever.

Holding back is a thing of the past.

I am doing this different; I am making change.

No more whispering, I have spoken up!

I use to work from the bottom, now it's time for the top!

I refuse to blow this off and skip town.

Forgive me for coming on strong, but you're my stopping point.

I came all the way back just for you.

Emergence

Just as great as a soothing song you get stuck in my head;
something special sums up who you are.
When you put your love in my life, I tend to live much better.
No one else in the world that I would rather have around.
I have what only your eyes can see.
Your feelings make me feel that intoxicating insanity!
Music whispers pleasures in my ears, while
your voice echoes love into my soul.
Tender describes your touch and fierce is your personality.
No need to prove anything to me, I love you already.

A Loss of a Gain

When do things change? Is it when we are fed up and are incapable
of enduring any more and decide to change things up? Or is
it when we have taken it so far that the only pattern would be
to drop everything, escape, and look forward to new? Looking
back is an emphatic no, but going back is an even greater NO!
The way the brain functions is completely opposite of the heart.
Smarts versus feelings of emotions? Interacting with the brain
and heart at the same time allows a consistent conscience.

What Do You Do?

Does distance determine how abreast we will be?
No matter how far you are from me, my life always
feels pure bedlam during your absence.
I am happy with what I am doing, but I know this
won't last a lifetime, nor would I allow it to.
I feel like my life is being held hostage because I
am around strays instead of my norm, you.
The life you are living is going as fast as the speed
of light, yet my life is at a standstill.
I am frugal just because of the life I am trying to gain.
We count the days and nights every day, because it gives
us hope that we are progressing, being made closer.
If I could escape right now and know that
things would be just fine, I'd leave.
I can't wait to love you, my angel, while we listen to beautiful music.
You are the story that I am mesmerized by,
a story engulfed with just you.

Espionage

Don't you trust in what I am doing?
Do you not know that you are included in everything I do?
This can't be a shock to you; you're embrace
has showered my entire life.
My feelings for you are written all over me.
My team is important, and you are my franchise player.
Making you fascinatingly joyous is my DEDICATION TO YOU.
Please say there is hope that still evolves here.
No need to wait on anything in life; I just continue to try with YOU.
We are going to the playoffs together; please don't look to trade me!
Remember God took everything from Job because the devil
came and told him that God had given Job everything.
God knew Job was faithful and could last through any turmoil.
Divine is your essence, and sublime is the
feeling of knowing that I have you.
That is how I feel about you being with me.
Starting a life with you, I knew that no matter what was given or
taken away from us, we were DEDICATED amongst each other;
more than a DEDICATED diva.
Say something clever!
Louder!

Turn the speakers up; this is the moment of unfading brilliancy!

Let us hear how your DEDICATION has marveled your life.

You are soaked into the grasping, acquitted minds from around

the world that are willing to let you vibe with them.

They nearly ran when your name was announced!

From your nonbiased opinion to your helpful, never-

fading attitude, you are the world's "Ave Maria."

Rosie the Riveter, yet you're poetic!

Your life is like a live hotline, and the world has never been let down.

Now that you have heard her sound, are you influenced?

More than a diva, works harder than any

man or technology-based clone.

State the facts, she is noticed around the world.

She gave you hopeful chances and held your hands to guide.

Although she is just one of God's amazing creatures,

she made sweet dreams beautiful, comprised of real life moments.

She protects everyone, so she is respected.

Her diamond keys unlock world hunger and racism.

Yearning for comfort with a side of listening,

she loves her position and only asks that you take from it wisely.

She will forever DEDICATE a true, keen

sense of direction until she perishes.

Men

They seem to break our hearts, yet they never forget us.
There is no erasing them, because they are a part of daily breaths.
They play that part in our lives, that special role.
Women risk so much to be with that one worthy man.
They put out everything yet deserving of us.

Pretenders ... Known To

Because they are ungrateful of their own lives,
they hate.
Because they do not look like you,
they hate.
Because they want what you have and desire to have what you own.
Loyalty was never one of their credentials, so they lack
and then linger by giving you unsatisfactory status.
You are self-made, and they lack self.
Did I mention they are looking for divine
involvement, and you are their hottest topic?
Your world is different! They want what is yours!
You have limits that go beyond the sky; they
are only going as far as their reach.
They look up, and you are there; they look low, and they're below.
Talk is cheap; therefore, you do not need money
to speak for you in those times.
You have hair that swings like Pocahontas.
Your life needs no departure method; you literally
execute everything you put your mind to.
Eating stars is just a thing you do naturally.
God is the only greater being.
Your life is creatively unique.
No matter how hard they try to change you, you will always be YOU!
They claim you as their favorite, but they mess over you like trash.
You are Kobe Bryant balling!
If they want trouble, just keep living!
What do you hate me for?
I know I am the only one that can stop me, not you!
It is out of my character to feed into your mendacities.
Feel free to hate on me!
I cannot take this any longer. Please let silence surround me!

Ain't Nothing Like You!

Connect yourself with me.

I like your skin.

I adore your short kisses.

I even like your hair!

Most of all, I see you as my sunset.

Tranquil, beautiful, well-built, and something

worth sharing; ain't nothing like you!

Today is great, and I am risking my all just to be with you.

The idea of having your attention curves every pain I ever possessed.

I hope we can keep each other.

I want to figure you out because I am curious.

I cannot dance around you any longer.

Your scent just drives me wild.

What a surprise this is!

Isn't this just natural?

You know for yourself what you desire.

I know what I need.

Be thoughtful, for I am a great plan.

No food nourishes me the way you do.

I crave your hands, for they hold the key to me.

Why? Cry! Lie!

For you to continuously relate me to your past is
not promising, and it makes my head twirl.
That has a huge affect on our progress.
Don't recognize me like the rest.
Why?
You may not know how to kiss me, love me, or talk to me,
but if you're still stuck back there, please remain.
Until you gain knowledge or sense to notice that I am
different, you won't find my love or get along.
You say I am the American dream, yet you
get caught up in your world.
Seeing me and not knowing me, then imagining that I am all yours,
is so redundant; because now you have me, and all you have to
say is what you always wanted to do with me, yet you have me!
Cry!
Actions portray realness; words portray lust.
I know you can always do without someone, but I
want you to allow me to be your completion.
Allowing my time to go by and be wasted is something people rebuff.
I am facing you, yet I know you can hurt me.
Lie!
Waking up is a blessing, and getting you to give me
your time is a fundamentally correct action.

I dedicate completion.

I want to be the completion instead of underappreciated!Dear Future,

Love is poison for its potency is strictly unknown.

The only difference is that it will not send you through a rough time.

Breaking news, my heart is on the floor.

Love, can you save me?

Will you make an effort?

Love, I need you!

You're the only one that can fix me.

My pace is set by you.

My way is your way.

I'm so interested in a relationship with you.

Love, you're so giving, you remain calm, and you keep me ready.

The power you have on me shapes my heart and

meets every need of love that I possess.

Why do bad things happen to good people?

This way you won't have to keep questioning me or this relationship!

I have been truly blessed all of my life!

At the same time, the question that they asked in the

movie I just watched applies directly to me:

"Why do bad things happen to good people?"

That's the story of my life when it comes to relationships!

Allow me to speak with you directly.

You're a diamond in this force field life.

You never were shown love like this, and

now I will shine in it with you.

Together we will make it better.

Let me get to know where you need help.

Life may get you down, but it won't ever tear you apart.

Look at change; see your change.

You have faith!

You are a man that prays; believe in what you say.

You know God is leading you through this.

If you refuse to let me shower you with lovely actions,

you won't ever breathe again through loves lungs.

I know you are flawless and sharper than anyone I know.

See what I am offering you, and then tell me if you can handle it.

I see this.

A man to have a wife that is with him through

thick and thin, ministry, calling;

standing by his side that honors him,

supports him, and just loves him.

When she looks at him she smiles, and vice versa.

The man looking toward his wife with honor, support,

standing with her, encouraging, and loving her is a beautiful

perfect scene. He protects her; she feels secure.

Because God is in that relationship,

he has brought it together perfectly.

Great and bad things happen to us all; don't let that be

your excuse for not making things happen with me.

Quit you're worrying and crying, baby; you can conquer everything!

Nothing You Can Say Will Change My Mind

The same excuse I gave for dismissing you is the one that
allowed me to lose my mind by giving up on myself.
I have exceeded the same type of man.
I am on my knees asking God to make a
point in all of this rambling chaos.
I have been caught up for so long, yet I never lost my way.
The time has come, and all I want to do is have him stay.
Closing my eyes gives me the chance to fall in love,
but once I open them, I don't believe it's true.
So, come be purple with me;
royalty, of course!

Deserving Joy

For the life of happiness, please smile!
And then realize that you can climb any
mountain that's set in front of you!
All it takes is effort.
Sometimes it is just easier to walk around them.
In all cases, cheer up.
Breathe with me, not against me.
Hold my hand and walk with me through the night.
Can I hold yours and say it will be alright?
What if I asked you to bow your head?
Would you trust me?
Only to tell you that I will still be your friend.
If that's what you want, that's what I will be,
but I think this is perfect.
But what about timing?
A face covered in a silent, still breeze,
but one must look deeper, because this is only temporary.

Falling in Love at a Dead End

Not even with all our might, the color of red;

I will never be worthy enough, yet you still bless me daily.

Not even close to being good enough;

victory is earned within your unchanging hands.

Testify and make my life clean!

I have been beat down, picked on; I have fallen so short.

Lord, your light shining over me makes every day on top of the world.

Daily I sit with you as if it is my last.

Every moment spent with thee completes my turning past.

I don't deserve you, nor do I speak of my own.

Rather peacefully, you have kept me.

Grace filled with mercies; it was you all along.

You that loved me, when no one else did;

you that spoke to me, when the floor and I met;

you that wrapped me in clothing full of glow, covering my sins.

If the rain is your tears, the shadows are my evolution.

Then I will be the ground that soaks up the drops to keep the

ground you walk on moist, yet just enough so that you do not

flood yourself in drowning away the life you have been given!

Can I Talk to You for a Minute?

If the ones you have come across were not the ones you desired,
may the Lord open your eyes to the man of God he has given
to you and rain down holy fire in every move you make and
sing; may the Lord shine, causing you to dance and sing.
May no man's will get in the way of our King; may your
heart be beautiful, and may your soul delight in Him.
In everything you do and say, may today just be sweetening;
so soft followed by kindness with soft-spoken rays.

His Love Song

Don't refer to me as another you see,
but rather, come rescue me from myself.
Would you miss me, not another from the rest?
But have me and try my mind.
We can do this together.
I'm on my way.
Let me give you what you need.
Don't be scared of me.
It's your heart; we can groove as long as you want to.
Let me, please,
give you a therapeutic remedy.
I'll show you fulfillment,
confidence; this is your best.
Ride with me; fly with me.
I will not play this tune, unless you allow me
to be your most excellent love song.

Excuse Me

No walls or person in between.
It's just wide open spaces, with thoughts of you inside of me.
I'll write the right, since the moment has turned around.
I want to see you for more than a brief moment; please
agree with me, and let us see if this is right.
Oblivious to the facial movements and secrets of words unsaid.
Today I would like to ask you, can we try just
one time to see if you are my forever?
Save the thought and soft tongue words
if only you are led by fictitious, tedious feelings.
We don't have to rush, for we have more than this night.
Honoring my heart's commands means I don't need
to break away from allowing you this chance.
I am not scared to go all the way with you.
Please don't play coy with me is all I ask.
There is nothing that can keep me away from you any longer.
The time is now, and you are more than Mr. Right Now.
You are the character in my cartoon, the color in my sky,
the sweet in my dessert, the rhythm of my heart.
Please, come on in; my door is open.
I love how you correct me, and I concur with the words you say.
I want to say so much more, but respect is what you expected.
But to lie and say that I do not feel the way I do
would only be immoral of me; would you still come to me?
To jump from now to forever is such a leap from end to end.
Instead, how about we have a heart that is filled fresh instead?
Let's see where this one goes, where we could end up. How though?
But distance is now behind us,
for nothing is too big for our God now!
I am in the right place at the right time.
For I know I am God's costar and your angel.
Finally, I can dive and land into pure elation.
Whatever the distance has in store for us, I am ready.
I am so anxious yet still trying to cope and focus,
for all I dream of is being near you.
This show is our show.

Count on Me

Life only expands for so long.

Make some rules up for yourself.

Never allow someone to not be forgiven in your heart on your clock.

Laugh hilariously all day and night!

Please never let your smile fade.

When life is extra rough, be grateful that you are still here

to dedicate yourself to something or for someone.

Burn people's eyes as if your soul is on heavenly fire!

Hand out specs to them since it's overly luminous!

Happiness is free, that you know.

Possess a glow that is unbelievable.

God has blessed you with eyes that sparkle when the light hits them.

Treat yourself to a spiritual lifestyle so that all you

can see are blessings working with you.

Definition

To understand the meaning of a sibling, talk to someone who has one.

To understand the meaning of time, speak to

someone who is fighting to live his or her life.

To understand the meaning of love, ask a couple

that still is in love after twenty-two years.

To understand the meaning of family, keep going,

because they give you reason to be here.

To understand the meaning of prayer, look at

your past and see where you are now.

To understand the meaning of someone that will

do anything for you, look at your soul mate.

To understand the meaning of a dream, try living it in real life.

And in closing, to understand this message,

you must have an open heart filled with humbleness and desire.

Knight, I love how your name looks when it's

written next to mine, Ann and Knight.

I love how you speak when I call; you smile because you hear me.

I love how your eyes shine when the sun glares its rays on yours;

I love how you share secrets after holding on to them for years.

Knight, go make your dreams a living testimony true.

I love to see the day when your calling finds you.

I'll find you.

Personal High

Exotic you are in the words that you speak.
Exotic you are in the way you move around me.
Exotic exhilarates the breath that you take.
Exotic are your lips, with mine wrapped in lace.
Exoticness electrifies our bodies bathed in silk, cream-
colored sheets that are made for passion, our passion.
From friends to lovers, we grew up.
Simply shining on each other's lives, my exotic
personality allows you to carry a part of me.
A lover's prayer is now answered daily.
You are the light of my life and you exceed my expectations.
With my head down and my hands held up so high, I
pray to God you will be my last first everything.
From the radiant love you show me, to your simple gestures
of joy, you represent the exotic islands of Costa Rica.
I cannot help but see you as the one for me; every time you
are around, I feel things that I know nothing about.
The way I feel inside is a smile away from an astonishing "I do."

Priceless

You are a monster that melts my heart, yet
I will never run away from you.
This love is meant for the two of us.
I'm going to grant your wishes.
You are that very special man that rules the world!
How incredibly intense is the moment of being in your presence.
No diamond can exceed your possessions of beauty,
nor could any pearl hide your marvelous heart.
The master plan between us is as touching
as us planning our first child.
Your exuberance fills up my mind with such shine
that every dull moment I encounter is brief.
You bring me to a breathless state of mind
when I am surrounded by you.
Let me be yours is my guarantee.
My intentions are epic; will you be mine?
Everyone loves to have what they can't have; well, I am here to say
that you are worth more than a want; you are who I wish for.
But before I spend any time or penny on you, I have to know that
you are here because you know this is where God wants you.

Enchanted Faith

You clear my air.
You fit right inside of my heart.
The very last could never escort such true
merciful calling into my soul's core.
I may have dreamt alone before, but now I no
longer have to face another lonely night.
If you feel this is real, we are real.
I am already in love with you.
I never choose to settle for good enough.
My heart speaks only to you and for you.
The glow is within the action of having you.
We should connect on a deeper level that is
beyond the surface of your normalcy.
Close your eyes.
Keep them opened.
Now once you open them, I want you to realize
that you have just received a miracle.
It may be small to you, but it's major to Jesus.

Self-Portrait

Litigious is not a trait my character lives up to.
The mental is my focus over the physical.
Me being selective with my decisions is not deprivation;
it's enrichment to how I break things down.
I have a secret that is so intriguing, it is allegorical.
I love to think that I behave like a human being.

Guts

The number of wins, the New York marathon, or even escaping a vicious highjack does not measure bravery. The real defining moments of bravery are so much simpler. They happen to be those times that you can only pass from thinking within; the moments of struggle when you are in the hot seat and decide not to quit because everybody else around you is negative and has already quit. Also, when you are around others and they seem to be doing the same "wrong" thing, and you show up with your "right" actions and stand alone. That one time when pushing actually keeps you alive and stumbling saved your life. You gotta believe.

Jocund

You're my angel.

Virtuous and faultless is what you are about.

Implausible is your delicate scent.

Trustworthy is one of your main functions.

Being a man is uncomplicated for you, but overall

angel wings place you above the rest.

You are so today and never to be ancient history.

To be in your existence is a blessing with ideal tranquility.

Having your attention remains anonymous,

yet calms me and shows me WHY.

You give me motive.

You are the raison d'être.

Unexpected is your way of living life but being shown

off is a thing of something that you are not about.

You're genuineness is what LOVE was made on.

Part 3:
A Love Song's Melody

Stop This World

Thirty-three days and thirty-three nights to go before I see you.

Six long years it has been since I was embraced by your presence.

We started as freshmen, and look at us now; high fliers!

I wish I could have been involved with your

achievements, but who else can come into my life and

make it feel like nothing has been out of place?

You've handled me.

I shouldn't have to wait for you.

Wait for you, love!

Love has only visited me once in my lifetime, and

ever since then, vacancy became known.

Our eyes were magnets when we were first met, yet our minds were

not advanced enough to build the courage to approach one another.

So unique is what I knew you were.

You also thought I was posh, foxy.

No matter our differences in paths, we migrated and

found out that we were closer than close.

This was never easy, but I never held you

responsible for not taking me away.

God was surely defining a moment of value for us.

What a good look this has become.

Who knew technology could feel so good!

From your "lay me down to sleep" voice to your structured,

impeccable intelligence, you elevate my life.

You were born a star and became my destiny.

Introducing myself to you was the best thing I could have ever done.

But if I only knew your name.

Number One

Happiness is what fills my stomach to cure my appetite.

Good conversations thrill my bones.

Holding hands with you fights off chaos.

Laughter delivers strength.

Eye contact gives my body chills that I could never forget.

My brain loves how you are always brand new.

Your loyalty exalts a pleasing presence.

What you do makes me proud.

Your prayers are harmonies.

Your imperfections are perfect to me.

The love you give, I crave.

Everything that involves you, I strongly desire.

You treat me so fine with divine actions that lead to our "I do's."

Yours truly is my aftertaste, when I think of my number one.

A Beautiful Sadness

Words are so profound, yet they diminish when the day begins.
Look for hope and confidence in a love that flirtatiously
burns with passion which will never die.
Believing that you will soon disappear from
my sight makes me a big mess.
I am torn up, because I am losing my soul mate!
The heart that was once a lost cause, you helped find.
We were supposed to last forever!
We're born to live and die together; now I must live alone!
I would rather die with you than live without you.
I do not want to die, but rather live with you in a home;
a life full of joy, peace, and love songs.
We shared these words for so long that have been sung to us at
last, but I want to move forward and share with you what I have.
Give me your hand; I would like to dance
with you through the night.
But if you refuse, then sadness is spelled right.
To speak from such distance and never hear your voice;
I will not give in.
The words you speak so gently will be so beautiful.
Sadness tries to fill the void.
I do not know what comes from this to be, but
we can start and see what we might be?
Beautiful sadness for a thought of what is not;
beautiful sadness for a success that is agreed,
but still cannot have;
a beautiful sadness indeed.

Focusing

Trying to focus when I'm around you is like trying to breathe
on a rollercoaster, falling from the face of the earth.
Something that is hard to do.
Insanely, fervently intoxicating with flavor; burning
up the insides of ever being close to you is the kind
of love that makes you stand to your feet.
Give me the key to life so I can breathe;
a key to hide inside of you, holding you.
Protect me;
your skin touching mine, allowing me to live.

Are You Ready?

But I'm not through.

I was told that hate does not transpire from home.

My head is where fate recedes and triggered emotions flow.

People are living lives like they are lost souls on vacation.

To make sense of this, I live fighting, but only

heighten my situations by being for sale.

Want to trade places?

My arms are trying to cast bundles of assurance

to those who have no one in their corner.

Always out of reach. The only hope for me is His unchanging hands,

for He knows I try so hard but I am only an imperfect being.

We need your flawless love, because you know I am going to fall.

You are never alone, and He takes you as is.

Homecoming Glory

All you have to do is let me in your life.
Questions arise about yourself, because you
are not aware or your own self.
Honestly, you are so confused about yourself
that your life is all a blur.
Do not listen to what you want to hear; learn to
explore outside of yourself and feel my presence.
Obedience, heard of it? Want to learn about it?
Life can be so pleasing, and every question you ever
had will be answered only if you seek me.
I never said that the sun would shine every day, but I assure
you that you shine regardless of your surroundings.
You will learn to know naturally that I will never
leave you, and you are not by yourself.
Take a photo of your life; do you like what you see?
I do not. This is not the plan for you, and I want you to try mine.
Talk to me, and let me show you that I am around.
I may be from Heaven, but my address is Universal Lane.
I made magazines for people to subscribe to, not to
contain foolish thoughts or live by them!
You know what happened last night would have
never happened if you sought me first.
Whatever it takes, I will do, but understand that every partnership,
relationship, friendship requires more than one soul and heart.
Follow me, and let me give you my cure-all remedy.
The only reason you have survived this far
is because I made it possible.
It's best that I stay.
Stand still and know that I am God.

It Is Well

Down and troubled?

Need to be loved?

How about a hug from your mother with a kiss from your father?

Never expected this did you?

Let's learn how to become an addict of triumph and not failure.

I know you; you know me.

Life can be your dream, but heaven is much nicer.

Figure out a way to catch a flight back to normalcy.

You are special; do not change, for there is reason for this brief.

Take a chance, have a rendezvous, head to

France; it's all in your actions.

Tell yourself something good; show yourself something better.

Come back together; let mirthful relations be

your number one cause and effect.

Prime yourself back up and see this through.

It is well with your soul.

Wow!

High of a Delightful Amazement

You might as well be placed on top of the world's tallest
pedestal, for you make this world what it is today.
As my aegis, you provide prosperity and much
character of fulfillment to my life.
You can get the best of me, because you helped pick up
my pieces. Regardless of what situation I am in, I know
that no weapon formed against me shall prosper.
Your spirituality has me praising Jesus for
prayers He has already answered.
I see how nicely designed your DNA is, which makes me
want to create another you with a mixture of me.
God has therapy for us that will help us solve all of our problems.
Let it go and just breathe.
Although you are spectacular, we were created by one God.
Soul mates, the reality that makes you want to stick with
that person without having to go a day without them.
My life has always been way ahead of what my eyes can see.
Does it astonish you with the way things always seem to happen?
Problems arise in life, and you always believe
they will never end, guess again!
Dreams are complimentary moments of reality, is all I can say.
Molding yourself as a whole with your imagination
can build your awareness to your surroundings.
Whatever duties you want to take on, do it in pure bliss!
Sometimes things taste better than what they look like.
Your mind is bigger than any galaxy; fix it up as its own gallery.
The brain does not require batteries; it has complete
control to function on persuasion.
You are the definition of character; rock to your best beat!
Jesus walks with you.

Passion of a Worthy Being

My cage has finally let me out!
What I have craved the most is what I have had
to wait patiently for my entire life!
You!
Enter and bring nothing but yourself.
Please do not fret, for I will never treat you like a
seasonal toy; nothing is better than US.
Previews are now obsolete, and you are my day-
after-day habit, and I am inside of you.
Swallow me whole and get familiar.
Your persona is so enchanting, and the life
we are now living is monumental.
I cannot wait to … but first, let me take this moment all in.
What a relief this is to really have you.
Don't you just like love, or love love?
I must warn you; this could really play with your mind.
Sensational is how you feel about this, and I can
tell you feel the same way about this as me.
I want you to touch more than my body, even though I
know what you are capable of, what I desire to inspire!
Feel me with your heart's beats.
Enter my mind and trigger my spots.
Set me on fire by your wholesome eyes.
Kiss my lips and make me scream.
Better yet, just lie down next to me and make love
to my mind without saying one word.
You can go deeper into my brain and swim around my soul.
Our passion is beyond sex here; it is the level we live our lives.

Outside of You

It's not that good without a second hand.
Imagine being that person you pass up daily
under the highway on the way to work.
Hear me.
Ever wanted to help them?
My guess is an emphatic no.
Always had it made, had a home, and had it all?
If you did not have what you had now, could you survive?
Would you care to survive the despair of being without everything?
Would you even heed to take a second look at your life if you
had funds that were not enough to get you through the day?
Envision being without a home?
Money flow?
Nobody with a heart for you or a willing hand to embrace you?
Laughter without joy?
How about not having any shoes?
Clothing?
Your necessities consisted of a chance to give away your body?
Now what would you do now?
Standing under that highway being passed by and
told NO for all of the days, twenty-four hours.
Does that sound like the life?
Of course not!
Homelessness is still not impressive to who you are, right?
Why is it all about money?
Life works around money.
Is life money?
Is money life?
Are you just a life with money?
Impartial person?
Not having that second hand, could you still cope?
Sit back and look at your life, homeless or homeward
bound; is it being lived or just standing still?
I bet you would not trade yours for theirs.

Our Lovers Prayer

For devotion, eternity, and you, this is my prayer.

I pray that my life is good enough to become one with yours.

I pray that your strength carries you through

the times you are without me.

I pray that the tears won't last through the years.

I pray that you can understand my mission.

The vow that I made with you will influence our lives beyond

any distance; we certainly will survive through anything.

The sun will shine over your life no matter how low you feel.

I pray that whenever you call, I will be by your side.

Faith will carry us; therefore, we will always have each other's hearts.

Loyalty is my prayer, and love is my ultimate promise to you.

My love for you is blind just as Jesus's.

It's unconditional.

I know God will answer this prayer.

Your smile lights up every place in my world.

Please do not ever stop its effects.

Having your trusts are solid grounds that we will never break.

Every ambition, goal, idea, plan, desire, or thought

you have, I pray that you reach it.

My final prayer is for you to take my heart

along with this ring and create life.

Amen.

It's You

Since the choice is mine, I choose to wake

up with you for the rest of my life.

I can handle that. Can you?

Every time I close my eyes to make a wish, I wish for you.

My colossal heart must have you.

Did you know that everybody loves you and

would go all the way to have you?

God is the only one that knows that I can't do without you!

I really do love you!

I am certain that I can make you happier.

From day one, I made things about you.

Please come here so you can see that I can handle you.

All I ask of you is you.

All About You

The thing about you is that you are beyond pleasant to my sight.

Your intellect is even spicier than the Cajun kitchens of New Orleans.

When it comes to being real, you are it;

nothing about you says phony.

I don't mind your physical being, yet you know

we are deeper into each other than looks.

You are that man that I want to come home to.

I know you will always be there waiting on me.

I am crazy about you!

You are crazy about me!

You are what I like and love.

I love it when you laugh.

I love how we sing the same songs.

I adore the things you say.

I love your thoughts when you feel stern.

I love when you want to spend your time with me.

I love the way you move and dance.

You know how to make me feel incredible.

You are so magnificent, its kind!

If we had one more day to live, I know exactly

what I would do and where I would be.

The loving is good enough to eat like a home-cooked meal.

You're the reason for this love that we share.

I love you.

Mr. Love Song

Talk about a man's thoughts.
Talk about a man's heart.
Talk about a man's vision.
Talk about a woman's thoughts.
Talk about a woman's soul.
Talk about a woman's strength.

Thanks to your songs, I can now make love.
I've listened to them all.
Thanks for your tunes, Mr. Love Song.
Thanks for the many vocals.
They show me love very easily.
Thanks for your tunes, Mr. Love Song.

Talk about the rare times.
Talk about a sweet scent worth losing your mind to.
Talk about a passionate night.
Talk about his love making, about his body.
Talk about your lively love life.
What about the ups and down?
What about the all-nighters?
What about the male ego?
Write your own vows to him.
Do lovers really last?
There is so much more than butterflies.

Thanks to your songs, I can now make love.
I've listened to them all.
Thanks for your tunes, Mr. Love Song.
Thanks for the many vocals.
They show me love very easily.
Thanks for your tunes, Mr. Love Song.

At times, lovers lose their heads.
A kiss and some high heels can change that.
I know that Mr. Love Song can't be an answer for everything.
Thanks for the dreams.

Thanks to your songs, I can now make love.
I've listened to them all.
Thanks for your tunes, Mr. Love Song.
Thanks for the many vocals.
They show me love very easily.
Thanks for your tunes, Mr. Love Song.

Part 4:
Doing it BIGGER

Yeahhhh
(Poetry night)

Everybody come on and feel this beat.
Come on in and feel it in the soles of your Nikes and Pradas.
Let lose to this sophisticated beat of moral hip-hop flow I have.
Let me make a rhyme or two with this and lock
the place down for the rest of the evening.
Yeahhhh.
Listen to me; don't be scared though, for this is only
the abstract aroma of a good fellows beat!
Everybody can jam to this.
You all came to my show, so I know you respect my flow.
Yeahhhh.
Let me know if you all wanna go to that feel-
good place, that real good place.
That place where you can have whatever you
like and be whatever you like.
Ahhhh haaaa!
Yeahhhh.
I know you all are cool with that, so let's get it going.
This is not a track for you to beat in your car; this is
more like my poetic lifestyle in forward motion!
Wait a minute; you all aren't feeling this yet?
Yeahhhh.
OK, let's bring the mellow back, and let me shout inside your
souls and make your ears blaze with the blessed of the blessed.
The rain sure is coming down now.
You all don't need to be scared of getting out
of your seats; let me feed off of you!
All this is called yeahhhh!
Feel this, folks.
I'm going to sing you a song that is meant to be on
repeat, due to you repenting for the remaining days
of your one time for your holy mind life.
Yeahhhh.
Visualize this abstraction of waves clapping to the beats of this song.
Listen to the cymbals as I fade into the background.
Yeahhhh.

Thunderstorm

Gratify my needs while I yell.
Living out here in this thunderstorm,
I can't take it any longer.
Withstanding you has washed me over.
Being out of the storm inside doesn't help.
I need protection for my broken views.
Rescue me out of the thunderstorm.

I can't take it any longer.
Withstanding you has washed me over.
Being out of the storm inside doesn't facilitate.
I need protection for my broken views.
Rescue me out of the thunderstorm.

I love you more than I ever knew;
scared to ever let you know.
My heart's been broken too many times.
I loved strong.
I let go.
Then I got let down.
What I know now was what I wished to have known then.
My mistakes have to teach me, lead me.
No longer will it keep me down.

Every time it rains, it fills;
continues to fall, to flow,
never ending.
Struggling to stay afloat;
once again I'm the victim of love.

Don't go and leave me alone.
Dying in this thunderstorm (this thunderstorm),
I can't take it.

Gratify my needs, while I yell.
Living out here in this thunderstorm,
I can't take it any longer.
Withstanding you has washed me over.
Being out of the storm inside doesn't facilitate.
I need protection for my broken views.
Rescue me out of the thunderstorm.

Oh, how I desire to show you love.
It kills me to let you leave unknowingly.
Needed you, desired you for myself.
Never let you see my pain.
I ran you away.
Why couldn't you see right through me,
and do something to help me reach my peak?
I'm living a 24/7 thunderstorm.

Every time it rains, it fills;
continues to fall, to flow,
never ending.
Struggling to stay afloat,
once again I'm the victim of love.

Gratify my needs while I yell.
Living out here in this thunderstorm,
I can't take it any longer.
Withstanding you has washed me over.
Being out of the storm inside doesn't facilitate.
I need protection for my broken views.
Rescue me out of the thunderstorm.
Stop leaving me behind in this harsh midst.
When the rain comes, so does a thunderstorm.
I always feel you before you come.
Please stay with me.

I can't take it any longer.
Withstanding you has washed me over.
Being out of the storm inside doesn't facilitate.
I need protection for my broken views.
Rescue me out of the thunderstorm.

Inscription Book

I choose you
I like you; you like me.
But we still can't be together.
I've got butterflies.
You possess the same feelings; too bad we can't feel them together.
I sit outside and think;
the way it would be if I had you.
I dream of only you.
This is what I do.

I sing out loud;
write our names with hearts.
Only my bedroom walls know how I truly feel.
Yeah, that's it.
Oh, just like that.

You just have no clue.
How hard it is to not have you when you mean so much to me.
The connection;
I want to tell someone, anyone!
Yet, all I can do is write the love in my heart about you.
Someday I've got to tell you,
I am in love with you!
Every time I've loved,
I've lost more.
Then I let it slip away from me because I did not speak.
No, not this time; I will not be sorry anymore.
It's going to change right now, today.
Take my words.
Digest what's been on my heart.
Listen while I write.

Have YOU Met THIS Woman Before?

Allow me to introduce you to her.

She will help you unwind to the point where it will never grow old.

She will show you that not only today is your day, but every day is.

She will give into you and desire all of your fancies,

make your life like a nursery of flowers in heaven.

She will make you feel like you can hardly wait.

She is every little thing that you could enjoy.

She will make you lose control, yearning to never let go.

She will relax your life, massage your mind,

sing to your heart, and love your soul.

She will deeply touch you like never before.

Open-minded with a soul of pure strength.

She will strike up conversations that are allowable on NFL Sundays!

Nothing can measure to her shine.

She is your cure and remedy.

She was conceived by your rib and will always be a part of you.

A necessary love is one of the desiderata in this woman.

She will add a pragmatic glow to the overall essence of your

vulnerability and share lengthy times of elation with you.

She will unchain your heart and still be around

if you crumble to the bottom.

Just right for you;

her presence is so inviting that you could never think twice about her.

She may not be perfect, but He designed her perfectly for YOU.

She is more than a first lady, a dreamy wonder, eye candy

of beauty, nice legs in a pair of heels, or a fantasy.

She is so real!

Rubbish- The Unedited Version

Time is expiring.
Stop making me wait.
I have to know.
Can we begin?
Why didn't I win,
Win with you?
Why didn't I win with him? You never came.

Photographs all over;
gorgeous, lovely eyes.
Please tell me;
can we begin?
Sought out with no response,
confused deeply,
searching for Levi, every day.

I'll love you,
even date you first.
Really, I'd date you.
We can make it a jovial day.
Remember the date.
Sweetheart, I want to date you.
We can go out on a date.
How does that sound?
Jovial day,
jovial time.

Your smile brightens the sun.
Night approaches; your glow is food for the moon.
I want to discover your cue in the darkness;
show you the right way, right there.
Like the night fades, you bring in luminary beginnings.
I am so solo, and I really crave it.
I am solo, and you're my favorite pick.
Come right here, right now.

Time is expiring
Stop making me wait
I have to know
Can we begin
Why didn't I win
Win with you
Why didn't I win him; you never came
Photographs all over
Gorgeous, lovely eyes
Please tell me
Can we begin
Sought out with no response
Confused deeply
Searching for Levi, every day

I'll love you
Even date you first
Really I'd date you
We can make it a jovial day
Remember the date
Sweetheart I want to date you
We can go out on a date
How does that sound
Jovial day
Jovial time

Your smile brightens the sun
Night approaches your glow is food for the moon
I want to discover your cue in the darkness
Show you the right way, right there
Like the night fades, you bring in luminary beginnings
I am so solo and I really crave it
I am solo, and you're my favorite pick
Come right here, right now

Time is expiring
Stop making me wait
I have to know
Can we begin
Why didn't I win
Win with you
Why didn't I win him; you never came
Photographs all over
Gorgeous, lovely eyes
Please tell me
Can we begin
Sought out with no response
Confused deeply
Searching for Levi, every day

I'll love you
Even date you first
Really I'd date you
We can make it a jovial day
Remember the date
Sweetheart I want to date you
We can go out on a date
How does that sound
Jovial day
Jovial time

Your smile brightens the sun

Night approaches your glow is food for the moon

I want to discover your cue in the darkness

Show you the right way, right there

Like the night fades, you bring in luminary beginnings

I am so solo and I really crave it

I am solo, and you're my favorite pick

Come right here, right now

You know I crave you right now.

Said I need you, baby.

You know I crave you right now.

Right here, oh.

You know I crave you right now.

Can't we make it a lovely day, doll.

Your smile brightens the sun.

Night approaches; your glow is food for the moon.

I want to discover your cue in the darkness;

show you the right way, right there.

Like the night fades, you bring in luminary beginnings.

I am so solo, and I really crave it.

I am solo, and you're my favorite pick.

Come right here, right now.

Who Defines Love?

What does it do to you?
Tell me when it's truly TRUE.
People of all creeds have
attempted to find it.
Share your meaning of love with me, never mind!
Let's just ride!

Love is when there is no more fight.
Love remains when you disagree.
Love's a light in a thunderstorm.
Who defines love?
Love is like the person you thought you never
had when all have left you alone.
Nourish me; help me survive.
Give me love for only one moment.
Who defines love?
Who defines love? Who defines love?
Who defines love? Who defines love?

Could it be plausible to say there is such?
Or am I kidding myself and being foolish with my own heart?
A lawyer would say
love could be a not-guilty crime with an innocent verdict,
in order for one to feel this way.

Love is my certificate to never lose.

No luck, just a blessing makes me realize;

full of myself, my real self.

Who defines love?

Love's like a long hug.

Keeps me content when it's only me.

Love is who I want with me.

Who defines love? Who defines love?

Who defines love? Who defines love?

Love is epic; it makes me happier.

I am done with my search.

You're the one I dig deep with.

Who defines love?

When the birds stop singing,

love is still flying around.

Finally, we meet.

You define love.

For the many times I've looked for answers,

love came to be easy. It's my best friend.

The definition?

Who defines love?

You do; you define LOVE to me!

Mona Lisa's and Air

Your love is worth more than the Mona Lisa and air.

What you need, what you desire,

let me be your provider.

Because your love amounts to more than the Mona Lisa and air.

You're the best thing to ever happen to me.

For every star in the sky, you have your own desires.

Keep living your dreams.

If you would let me be your Forrest Whitaker,

you could be my Queen of Scotland.

Audition in my movie; you can be life, girl.

Take your talents to the sky, for it's the limit.

Halle Berry, still looking for the next man;

caramel chocolate, but baby you've been neglecting.

Could I be more inviting?

For there is a true-life sentence that's linked to my heart.

You're just that debonair; you're so very sexy.

Once you open up, all I can see is you.

Being so right, you could never break my heart.

Telling me all the good things; just let me be your life.

Between you and me, we would always end up right.

Mona Lisa, delicious kisses, every time we're around.

Your love is worth more than the Mona Lisa and air.

What you need, what you desire,

let me be your provider.

Because your love amounts to more than the Mona Lisa and air.

When we were down and out, we'd bicker,

fight, and leave the love song alone.

Overall the thunderstorms ended, and we're living right.

What a friend you've been to me.

Meant to be, you stayed true to me.

You were blinded by your ego, not realizing that I was your hero.

Saying you need to relax, you were technical about everything.

Wasn't amused by a breakup.

Take a flight wherever you were.

Make it all better; make us work.

Sunny days surrounded you, while the cold got a hold of me.

Stood strong, we couldn't bear any defeat.

You sat and saw me cry at your front door.

You weren't hearing me.

Took me in and held me tight, promised

me everything would be alright.

Be mine again; let me bear all that you care to dare.

Working for the key to my heart, you reap what you sow.

Charge it to the game; we have conquered our first time.

Flight 271983

Drained and unresponsive are YOU.

I find it hard to say that your life is being lived.

Your ways are missing.

The life you live is indecent; deep down you already know this.

Facts of your past are nameless.

You are your own little secret, and you live to keep it hidden from all.

Speculation arises every time one cares to get close to you.

The love you share is only self to self.

Who wants to know you is of no concern; for

you'd much rather sit solo, independently.

To you nothing is off beam, to everyone else there's apprehension.

Who do you trust? Who trusts you?

Waste of time is your lock and key to the world, for the crack in

your heart is your explanation, for your testimony doesn't run over.

If it were up to you to help turn the world right

side up, you wouldn't care to contribute.

A wondrous light, capable of captivating,

suspenseful interior, phenomenal exterior;

like an ensemble you are only heard by a selective few.

Mellowed out with no sight of distractions in his highness.

So resolute, desolate, and rue.

Selfishly devoted to self with a luster of

confidence that is untouchable.

Never to deny the will to change for this individual's past
is a blank black and white, for there is nothing written.
This individual is the type that is all about him.
One would sing that change was only for a dying heart, yet dancing
to your pace makes your life miraculous like a Paris night.
Being near this individual feels like a hideout
in an UP alley with no venture.
The hands of this individual are lukewarm yet possess a fragile feeling.
Enchanting appearance, awkward couplet, paper feeling,
secure sensibility, sugary residue, rainy day eyes, fierce focus,
solo, skeptical, careful daily with the voice of no psalm.
A breeze if you were to pass this individual by
dawn but later a slick fish in the sea.
A momentary bounce that would make you feel
embraced with the price of ambiguity.
In this individual was something old, polished, painful, a scent
of prolonged existence, out of sight, and merrily never seen.
This is all he has made known, a never-ending mixture of feelings.
But is it really better to battle to know YOU?
I wanted to be your favorite girl, give you the world and more.
No favorite girl of yours;
a closed door would best represent you.
This was a radio message to my love song.
Now, tell me who you are!

Part 5:
Lunch Specials

You Choose the Title

Each breath taken, not heard by your ears, is a waste of air.
Embracing the magnitude of sacrificing,
I say unto you, am I becoming a better man?
God's hands are unchanging.

He forgives sins.
Your heart or mine, it is a win.
Often tempted to fall into the rapture of love, barricading your
feeble emotions into a pit of a bittersweet and what if's.

Searching lifeless in an ocean of broken hearts,
j'espère you soon find a mend.
If not, give me your location, and the search shall begin.
Let us lay like lovers lay.

Our souls adjust to the heat rapped in an incubator of
emotions, blinded by fear due to our eyes being new
to what God calls life, but for us it is called love.

From God is time, my angel; I have one question: do the
gates of heaven open simultaneously or at different times?

Pedal to the Floor

Pedal to the floor.

The days are turning into hours.

Days ago when things felt right, things were clearer.

Now you are gone so far.

How can I keep you near?

Passing time feels like a sudden pitfall to a fast death.

Would it be too much to ask for?

Won't you come back?

Play my favorite love song and declare your heart!

Another minute and I'll be a solemn grunt of a past "I love you."

Oh, my love, if begging will help,

I'll give you that and more!

Don't trade this in for a case of another bad romance.

No single being compares to your effects.

Realize.

Thank you.

Time

Getting rich doesn't solve dreary nights.

When you are out, are you really there?

Your handprints, are they going to let you start over?

Time is pushing; you are getting older!

Breathing seems to last even though your strength isn't healthy.

There is no way you can make a plan that

could be done all in one night!

Even though things are going as right as they

can, something is bound to blow!

Cradle your soul, for that late-night call can detour your stance.

eBay can't sell it to you; Amazon couldn't

find it; Google couldn't discover it!

Here the light comes, ask for it to stay this time.

Him vs. Me

His insides spontaneously combust as he
hears the rhythms of my voice.
You don't even have to try when it comes to loving him.
Everything with us just happens.
The heart is the main piece that satisfies this hunger.
He releases his feelings from his soul and
mounts them on to my heart.
My all-star is his position; first, is his place.
Walking up to him is no mind-set; it's purely impossible to lose him!
In France it's *mon amour.*
Something I know is that he takes his time
as he makes love to me in Houston.
He thanks me for the times.
I thank him for sharing his love.
He is the property of the Oktoberfest, for he stays sober.
Guidance is free, so he makes huge donations.
He will never leave you unguarded like the Bermuda Triangle!
Making magic is when he is on the hardwood, for it's
his studio of expression that never backs down.
Shakespeare in motion with blood, sweat, and love.
Without any fear, he is who I claim.
He is me and I am him when we get closer together.

Part 6:
The Best-Case Scenarios

I've Never Witnessed

My eyes have never seen you.
I've never witnessed the shape of your eyes.
I've never witnessed the smell of your flesh.
Beyond your physical presence, your intellectual
attributes have never been seen.
I've never witnessed the strength in your stance.
Your heart who sings instead of beats, never witnessed.
I've never witnessed the grip your hands would
have on me while you kissed me.
To daydream about it shows me that you take your time.
I've never witnessed your face when you wake
up under God's gorgeous sky.
We could definitely go all day and night long.
I've never witnessed the difference between bitter and sweet with you.
Electronically inclined, connected to your hard drive, best
wallpaper ever placed on your screen, still never witnessed.
I've never witnessed you playing by the rules in the game.
So happy to see you playing your part as if I'm your entire team!
I've never witnessed the stain of a tear on your fresh face.
My heart is what is starting to care; have you noticed?
I've never witnessed you in a crowd of good intentions.
Every day that ends, I am still able to indentify you.
I've never witnessed you under pressure as if you were unworthy.
That's just never how it will be.
I've never witnessed you losing yourself to
gain another's uninviting attention.
You would never trade places or take back the
time that you gave me to show me love.
I've never witnessed you collapsing, which is nearly relaxing.
Being with you allows me to never lose, but actually enjoy you more.
I've never witnessed you at the bottom, but I do
know what you look like from the top.
I've never witnessed a mogul of inspiration,
until you.
You are beautiful, and I am a witness.

SOS

Still young and have developed many tears.
This broken heart couldn't stand a chance against a cold ego's blow.
Jesus, please bring me higher, closer to another lover.
Mistakes can't be made twice.
But it's those lonely nights;
those have me going against myself.
Asking for love, requesting its presence;
then he appears.

Claiming that he heard my SOS.
But then I said that I was waiting patiently,
requesting love, asking for its presence.
But wait, before you go any further, let me ask you this:

Do you want to show me this, or better yet, just kiss?
You know that's not the way to get to my heart.
But for you to leave without a fight, you've
got to know that's not right.

Dated the players and the foolish;
seen many boys and ones who couldn't carry the torch home.
Been betrayed before, but I won't let that happen again.
Give me you and crave not my fame.
But if you can't make up your mind about me, keep walking past me.

Please don't even waste our time! My time!
Every time someone is introduced to you, you have no way
of knowing if they will leave you speechless or breathless.
But I know who you are.
You are bigger than any hype; you are so good to me.
Don't let me wait for you anymore.
Come to me; it's us against the rest.

Two of a Kind

Loving this day, shared as one, our souls connected soon, we will learn of what has become. (C)

Enjoying the emotion, filled with nothing like extortion, we have yet to see the true revelation. (D)

Allowing self-acceptance for the sake of love, a voice soon to be filled from the heavens above. (C)

Nearly a missed opportunity with a hint of like, yet involving each other's similar delights; pure high. (D)

To be his is to be at the top of the mountain peak with full access to bliss; with no pondering doubt of disbelief, he stands so still next to me. (D)

Nights turn cold, days are stretched, praying as one that our emotions be blessed. (C)

I stand so still, because I know that you are rare; your smile, your skin, I know you will double my pleasures. (C)

If asked who he is; she claims him as her heart, her main attraction without any doubt. (D)

The time he shares is like a moment gone great with a perk of a kiss that is soothing enough to catch your fall. (D)

No need for doubts, I no longer fear the unknown; I will cater to your weak and better your strong. (C)

While catering to my weaknesses, he influences me beyond life's surfaces and vacates me near his soul. (D)

Like the rocks mashing against the seashore, with the same thrust as a honeymoon; her heartbeat matches mine; never shall I flat-line. (C)

A sight for sore eyes, he can heal the sick and give hope to the blind. He is never a return to sender! (D)

In her armor for protection, her relief from pain, the fuel of her lighter without her then there can be no flame. (C)

His love loves me; his eyes are addicted to mine. His hands are all over me; he fulfills me and takes me higher than the cities limits. (D)

He is who I adore, the one I yearn to live with. He entices me, for that he is colossal. (D)

Everything about him says, "Keep going," but if you care to find better, you'd better deny, exit, lose sight, and take a hike out south. (D)

No limits are meant, as they will never be reached. I sing, she listens, and the rhythm of love taps our feet. (C)

A dedication comes with his relations, a request is made upon arrival; if you want him, simply tell him. (D)

I will ride west, so that the sun sets in my sight. I must say, thus far this has been a wonderful quest. (C)

Just like a flower that blossoms in the summer breeze, his presence exhorts a potent sense of relaxation. (D)

For this wonderful quest is something that I could taste for the rest of my life. (D)

Entropy of tranquility with reality behind; what is understood does not have to be defined. (C)

Entropy is energy and tranquility is calming, so when we love, we're making straight A's! (D)

Before there were you, I was a book without words, no meaning. Now that you are here, this book will have a happy, fulfilling ending. (C)

I'm a tidal wave of endearing emotions. If you knew I was with him, you'd see that we're happily even later! (D)

I use to be without. Love use to be so cold, so tart. But now I'm for certain that I was only seeing what was behind me instead of what was in store. (D)

Your emotional waves are soon to be calm; there is always light shining after your storm. (C)

Please rescue me out of this storm with your embracing arms of natural strength. Take me away with you, and I promise you won't be missing out! (D)

I notice your glow of who is to blame. Whoever it may be, your crippled emotions should use him as a cane. (C)

I want to kiss you, hug you, and feel your eyes. (C)

Show me your love that so many have denied. (C)

I desire his lips, for his mouth knows nothing but ultimate pleasure. To hug him would be a crime, for I want a life sentence. To feel his eyes watching me makes me feel more beautiful than anything that has ever touched me. To receive his love is like flying while walking. (D)

Fly, my angel, extend your wings with pride. Glide to my heart; I promise to let you inside. (C)

Keep going. Please. (D)

*C: Calvin Watson
*D: Danielle Deckard

162

Unexpected

Love has been so hard to find, hard to capture, receive, and keep.
When it came into my life, it came unexpectedly.
I never knew that you would become the one
who I wanted to last forever, live-forever.
For your love, I made a promise of truth to show you who I was.
A month ago, you and I were totally unknown to each other.
Now we cannot be separated or away from one
another longer than the second hand of a clock.

Your heart is more than beautiful; it's a promising gift of life, my life.
Being out here all alone, without a trace of love or
companionship in view, you came about, around.
After only one conversation, I grew attached, hooked!
"Gotta do it bigger," I said.
There is no one more important to me.
You have to see through me.
My day without you was a war zone in itself.
How ironic, because that's my current address.
You are now my heart's biggest aficionado.
I will not hide. I am in front of you; take me, choose me, pick me.

Your heart is the most important item I could obtain.
The facts of life are now the fun things of life, our lives.
Never to ask me for anything but to desire the song in
my voice daily were your biggest dreams come true.
Sincerely yours without any further ado, I would
never show you the pseudo side of anything.
To walk around with a glow that was given to my soul and
sprinkled on my body had your signature all over it.
Every moment that we spend apart makes me desire
you more, for I know that this will never end.

Out of all the pleasures and jocund feelings you give to
me, your enigma kicked up and presented itself.
Why was this happening again? The most
serendipitous part was not over.
Posh was who I learned, yet you mentioned being insalubrious.
Please don't hide yourself from me!
Why did you wait until I fell in love with
all of you to give me a choice?
Claiming to have something that could harm me, yet
you're too scared to share what it is with me.

I could never lie to you! Why do I feel like
you played a role with my heart?
Who are you, and what have you done with my January 9th?
Do you think that this should have been discussed
from the beginning conversations?
You nearly blew me away with your tip-top spirit
and a diverse heart was your response.
I never lied to you!
You are not safe to my existence.

There's nothing that's worse than losing you.
From a distance, I can still see our future.
Is this true? Unexpectedly, I became victim of a distant love.
There are too many signs in front of me that point to
me and not you. But you just turned them all off!
With my only heart, I need an answer. Life is hitting me in the face!
If you can't tell me WHAT, tell me WHY!
I am singing this song to you.
Let love be!

The Only One

Because of you, I am the only one.
Since I met you, I became your only.
To fight against space and distance is our
threat, but you must keep holding on.
The results aren't clumsy; they show that strength holds us.
Everything we have right now is stuck in an ongoing whirlwind.
You seem so real to me.
Yet, I can't reach out and touch who you are.
How you doing?
My soul is having desire attacks, because it wants
your love so badly every time you walk by.
Before you disappear, allow me this one chance to hold you.
For years I knew you would appear before my eyes.
Finally, you've come around, and you're more
than I could legally dream of.
You are more than a moment; you're a luscious lifetime keeper.
Love can't pass me by forever, so please don't
sail away without your captain.
Now the sun is setting slowly, increasing its
chances of sharing the sky with the moon.
Stand under the light with me; miraculously make
love to my soul, for this is our moment!
I can see the moon's twinkling effects as it shares its luminary.
The sun has drifted away, for its destiny is no longer around.

Finally, we can be together and be each other's only one.
All you must know is that we are real and will
never pass if we fall short of each other.
Just like the sky has an end, you and I shall
never be beyond our destiny.
Tell me if my love is enough to keep you around.
Don't miss this moment to realize WHO I am!

My only one, that's who are you. This will be what WE do: admire
the earth and cater to the animals and human kind, frown on riches,
provide sustenance to any and all, share your earnings and help,
overlook the bitter yet not the sweet, question God never, live with
patience and act on it, applaud what's real and not pseudo to man
and its kind, work vicariously with the righteous never to discover
a diploma, old, and underdogs, indulge in the dreams and exhale
through every moment given to a season, discover reality from a
brain rather than a rectangular wave box, mom and dad, and the
rev, ceasefire and think with your head and reason with your soul
in all that you need, and your body will be a love song with the
sweetest harmony of charm and addiction that will cherish on your
face and light your God-given glow in every area of your existence.

A Prayer for the Creative

Imagine with me.

Are you ready?

The time of your life;

preparation for your destination,

where you could never forget the Savior.

It's late in the day; Jesus is lurking the city.

He is fulfilling the laws and blessing those who do not mind.

The strangers have hot tears; the weary stand thanking him.

Not one could ever forget what He has done or will do.

He is who we think about.

The only that has paid his dues in full.

Life is not important without the possibility of His great pursuit.

You need more.

From A to Z, He will catch you, relate with you.

What's not to love about Him?

He's the reason for the moon and even the blues.

Don't you know better?

Didn't you hear how he does hearts?

He loves you even when you think He doesn't.

Want another chance?

What No One Can Take: That "Indefinite" Feeling

Seeing a being so lavish that could obviously touch your mind
mentally from a distance makes me yearn beyond the galaxy for you.
Mold yourself with me, and share your inspirational duties with me.
Let me take you on board; lend me your
hand, the entrance is out back.
Wait … can't you hear that?
That's the soundtrack to our newfound love life.
Do you like what you hear?
Every day that I see you, I wish you were mine.
Knowing the unknown makes us known.
No coincidences, just opportunities.
I just cannot let go of everything that is living on my mind.
No need to put up a fight or get your attention.
Right now you are here, close to me, natural, but later on,
you will be where you would never dare to leave.
I don't deserve to share you, but does she desire
you so badly that tomorrow doesn't have to come,
because you're all that a life needs in a day?
The future that I will never know kills me daily:
to be yours, all yours.
It's so obvious that you're no longer available.
But I am so wrong!
From this moment on, I'll keep looking back on yesterday.
That unknown feeling, take it away, for I am not at ease.

The Best-Case Scenario

Like a rush that you receive when you've discovered that one;
it is like living on love's freeway with a miraculous no-traffic zone.
Sometimes it is easy to see that it's a beautiful thing.
The writing is on the wall, so open your eyes.
You may not find this again.
Whenever you see me, you are stunned as the
life of the party stands before you.
Reality, the second best person you should know.
You're my only man, and I am your only woman.
There's a reminder.
Let me get to you; now pause.
Because I'm the definition of recognition and insistence.
Exactly, they don't make them like us anymore.
The best-case scenario is all things through Christ Jesus.
Are you serious?

Part 7:
Completion, Edition 2

Introducing a New Word:

Poetify (poh-et-a-fy)

Adjective

1. Act of being poetic.
2. When a great poet creates a structure of fabulous words that represent fascination of poetry, rhyme, emotion, or feelings.

Origin: 2009, Houston, Texas

Don't Blame It On

It's time to trade this daydream in for a life.
Her writes are meant to be tattooed in your heart.
The voice in her is etched on the outermost
part of your life, your soul.
Wait a minute; I am not done yet.
Her style is passion, its effortless; she is one who is irreplaceable,
pretty practical, and overall a downright classic!
The lady behind this write does not demand attention for
the weekend, her company is always at the door; but do
remember if she needs you, she will send for you.
Can you even compete with her? With all this?
No playgirl ploy, but she knows how to lay them down, lay them out.
No quick comfort, she gives you everything you need.
Wifey is her role, and she will go hard for you.
The cravings of love, loyalty, and respect are
included in my daily thoughts.
Twenty-seven years old with everything, yet needs more.
How about I have you chase her?

Waking Up in Reality

This morning is a major challenge, for last night was super amazing, and I just went to sleep an hour ago! I went to the office in downtown Taji, Iraq, and they played *"Party Life"*, while one gorgeous man put moves on me like NASCAR. It felt like I danced for hours with him. After that, I checked my emails, and people were wondering when am I going to go home to stay for good. They had me thinking about the record *"Slide Show."* However, what can I say, my life is just recordable. One thing though, I do not live for them; I live for Jesus lavishly. I would rather be jamming *"I've Got You Under My Skin"* by Frank Sinatra or *"It's Love (That I Feel)"* by Ryan Leslie from that special man. Speaking of men, did you spot Lloyd on the red carpet of the MTV Music Awards? For sure, I just wanted to sing *"Heaven Sent"* to him whenever we meet. Now if that does not work for him, I am clueless as to what else to do to get him!

(Laughs)

I just purchased a new Mediterranean house in Houston, but it will be a while before I get out there. But when I do get there, I will hit up Galveston Beach. I want the DJ to play *"PYT"* when I come through. One thing about me, I am always visualizing about hot weather and men excessively. The moment I noticed a gem, *"Diggin' on You"* triggered my hypothalamus. It's time I stop with the daydreams and catch this power nap. Definitely, *"Voyage to Atlantis"* will take me out. What a daydream this was.

A Chronicle of Expression

Sooner than later, you will be smarter than this.

You are the type to show them how to feel.

You can be the best he ever had.

Just a little bit before they document; no, this isn't lusting for life.

In uptown you are unstoppable; keep that face on.

Break a tibia, for the calming of His healing will soon

capture your damages, and they will digress.

Take the night off; you have the option.

Ladies and gentlemen, this concludes this game!

So Far, So Right

Pulling up to the stadium in my Maybach, my driver realizes that
they are directing us to another area, so we have to take a detour.
So far, so right.
I feel a little iffy from the night before, so I ask that my agent
makes sure the paparazzi does not use their flashes.
So far, so right.
Time to get out and head inside, thoughts going through
my mind are, it took me twenty-seven years to get here
and to feel that everything I did was worth it. It didn't
kill me; it made me live, and now I must have it all!
So far, so right.
I suppose you would like to see your dressing room and see
what fine garments we have set out for you tonight.
My reply, "Let's get live, for this is my moment of success."
So far, so right.
Forty-eight hours ago, my reality set in; now
that I am here, I realize I fit in.
So far, so right.
Clothing never made me get here.
Money only helped me feed my hands.
Cars never were as flashy as my inner persona.

Truth is what I tattooed on my hand, which
had it buzzing like a beehive.
So far, so right.
Dolce and Gabbana or Marc Jacobs were my choices.
So far, so right.
Marc Jacobs it is, where the stilettos resemble strawberry
shortcake, for they are that smooth and sweet.
So far, so right.
High heels are my foreplay, which I will use
as I strut to receive my victory.
Grand finale: wait, this is nothing but a daytime
photo shoot in the islands of Tahiti.
So far, so right,
Dressed up like J. Lo, I think to myself once again,
faith is hope and it sure looks good on me.
He is my greatest story.
So far, so right.
Click, click is the sound of my stilettos; thump, boom, boom,
bam, thump are the sounds of my humming heart.
One more breath, everything is about to go my way; the door opens.
So far, so right.
Congratulations, you are successful and welcome to the
award show of freedom and promise of sorrows no more.
I will father you and adore you.

No Thinking Small

The vibe is just known, for it always says we are correct.
That someone you were before you came into my life,
found me, and complimented everything that was me.
Love is how we put up with each other,
and reality is what we play with.
Perfection is how we see God, not ourselves, for we are his mini-me's.
You are the one that sees joy through all
this Seattle rain that we endure.
To watch the feet of our everyday moves would
confuse a newlywed couple, but we know it for the
better, because it says more than just a walk.
Early February is when you came to me, and late
October is when you dedicated eternity into no longer
being my costar; you became my final quarter.
We play no games, so any overtime is obliterated.
You are young, particularly handsome, utterly irresistible, unworldly,
and sincere, yet you are able to discover the world's ken.

Incredible

Living in the gray area,

Houston, Texas, born and raised.

Purchased for a price that no man could have ever paid,

for that she is worth.

There is not enough money in the world to repay.

It took one special man to win her heart, to win her soul.

No, there is no other man; there is only Jesus.

Salutations ... I Am NOT Through!

I brought you completion.

Before that, you thought you were running out of time.

Clearly, you knew very little about your blessings,

and that it is well with your soul.

Now, we may not be clear about when the world is going

to end, but we know what we know, and what we know is

whatever you desire to do, do it now, and do it swiftly!

I proclaim with no presumption.

In 2092, the magic of that moment is going to catch us by surprise.

There is something in the song that is more than a song.

Hold on, for this ride will lead you; and attach yourself to a state

of holding on, for its glow will only shine brighter with time.

Most people will be mad that you aren't with them, but hey,

that's the story they weren't meant to live in or with.

Everyone lives, time always passes, words always run out, but

actions represent expressions that go far beyond any measurement.

Do remember this psalm, for it will surely change up the pluck

of your guitar; it's a welcoming note that always catches your

attention and allows a song to be considered your favorite.

Generation Y gave you independency and let you

see the smarter side of life, technology.

Doesn't it seem like you should stop running away?

Make the best out of this moment; you can't

ever be considered a winner if you quit!

Never wave your flag or give in or up.

Lala.

Part 8:
iROCK, a.k.a. Iraq

The World's Prevalent Terra Firma: Iraq

If you are not fortunate enough to visit or live in Iraq,
allow me to welcome you to stay or compliment you
with my experiences of this mammoth sandbox.
Being accurately correct, visualize this picture of
Iraq as I try to paint it with my keyboard.
Somebody opening and closing the door behind
me sprays me with a load of dust.
Dust mixed with dirt equals filth!
There is no escaping the dust in this place; it infects
everything, leaving a film that never seems to come off.
Isn't it exciting when truth is told about how holy the
land of Baghdad is which evolved from Babylon.
Let me inform you that these details may scratch your skin
and leave the shower basin dark brown once you exit.
Everything is tried in Iraq, even suicide; in fact, they prefer it!
Essentially we are all human beings, whether
we hail from Texas or Ohio.
The vision of a child is of a scopes eleven-inch
chamber, where its eyes are focused on everything that
moves; no one is even safe around their kind.

No exceptions.

You know there's nothing like a day at the beach with

black sand, but the sand here is only black in color

from a bomb's remnant of last night's battle.

Is Iraq's experience hurt or holding it over itself?

Who will save the souls of this land since it is past out of control?

Iraq may not be the USA's direct neighbor, but

they sure do feed off one another.

Let's expose the scars of Iraq.

Satisfaction is not guaranteed; therefore,

relaxation is a thing of the unknown.

Money doesn't talk, but smoke speaks for itself.

Whatever they want to do they shall.

The sky cries blood, for the sands are nothing

but irritations to its everyday presence.

I have listened to the life of the Iraqi's wants; someone

supply these people with independency!

You can send your troops; set up camp!

However, they will not back down!

Please never ask them why they live this way.

What a harsh part that's filled with fight or flight; how muddled.

Rich Off Dirt
(A personal experience)

Day 922: Here I go again; putting myself on the line again,
for I am still in Iraq, the city of Tal Afar that hides behind
unripe mountains with a constant vapor of dust.
"Thank you, Lord," is my response, as my Motorola
Crimson Treo's alarm is going off as 5:15 a.m. goes live.
As I turn on my music, I talk to God thanking
Him for another day of life.
I sing and dance my way into my clothes, but first I freshen
my face and trigger my brain into clever mode, so I can
make sure this newfound day is a glorious day.
Opening the door to be greeted by a whiff of dirty, foul-smelling,
orange glaze of dust, I close my mouth and ask God to put His
hands on me while I make my way down the rocky road to work.
I walk to work reciting Psalms 27, for it excites
me and puts tonic in my steps.
Before I open the door to the office, I ask God to lead
me, for I know the devil is strong around me, but His
limelight is extra strong and will never go unnoticed.
The office is secluded and hides behind several concrete T-walls.
T-walls are made of concrete; they are shaped like
tall, rectangular pieces of Trident gum, yet they are
supposed to keep us safe if we ever are attacked.
My office is a wooden crate that is long in length and
short in width. It has no windows and two doors.
Its color is very dull, and its overall appearance
is screaming, "Remodel me!"

Climbing a set of three steps, I open the office door to
be greeted by fairly old strangers, my colleagues.
"Hello to all," is my response, as I make
my way to my uncluttered desk.
As I sit down in my chair, I say to myself, "Time to check emails!"
"Who wrote me today?"
"Who loves me?"
"Who has thought of me?"
Before I can even get into my emails, the daily meeting must start.
We are given our daily assignments via email.
I take my daily bread, too, for I will need it.
As the meeting is coming to a close, I sit there unworriedly waiting
for my chance to get back on my laptop and check my emails.
Sensational!
An email from my mother; she is a reference of
beauty; she could sale sand to a Bedouin.
As seven o'clock comes, I am already ready to get off
work, yet I know it's only time to go eat breakfast.
Of course, we have no fresh fruit on the side type of
meals, but cereal is my preference of dining.
Walking back to my room to where my cereal awaits me, I am passed
by empty buses that head to make their journeys to drive in circles
all day long as they pick up soldiers and take them around the base.
Concentrating on walking over the rocks, I picture
myself flying to my room, for every step I take makes
me just want to yell, "Get cement around here!"
I think to myself, I wish things were a lot more pleasant out here;
kind of a like a delicious banana split covered in fudge; sweet!

Entering my room, I take deep breaths, for it smells so
incredible I could just float away on its aroma.
Time to eat some cereal and get out of here.
Special K with soymilk, the breakfast of this champion!
Before I head back out on my same route, I brush my teeth
in peace. As I pour the bottled water over my toothbrush,
I think to myself, "I cannot wait until I can turn on the
faucet and use the water that comes out of it!"
Drinking the water out of the faucets is not a prophet,
for its non-potable, yet we bathe in it!
Time to head out; let me check my attitude and say, "Let's go, Jesus!"
Walking back over the rocks to get back to work, my mind
and heart tends to chase off every negative thought I have.
Although work is considered life to most people out here,
and all they do is walk back and forth each and every
day doing the same things, they indulge themselves in
jealousy; it is nearly over for them, is what I think.
Pure nonsense and nuisances; let me call victory
over this day before I begin work.
LSA 9 is my mission for today, marking the
CHU's is what I have to accomplish.
A CHU is a mobile container used for offices or living quarters.
Arriving at this unfamiliar area, I walk to the first
area, where I will begin to justify my work.
As I open my ebony paint marker, an Iraqi soldier with a huge
smile greets me. He says "Hello" to me, but of course I could
not understand him, for he spoke in his language of Arabic.
Working diligently on the CHU's, approached by another
Iraqi soldier saying, "You look Iraqi; where are you from?"

"The United States," was my response.

Not sure how he felt about me after I told him where I
was from; I was still an unusual suspect, not royalty.

An Iraqi soldier said calmly, "Please come inside."

Inside my head I told myself, "Don't be afraid, go for it."

Entering this tiny room that is filled with one TV, two
beds, and an untidy refrigerator, I take my eyes off its
unsanitary appeal and focus on the walls, for they are filled
with huge portraits of bright sceneries and animals.

This is where they got their joy from.

These were photos of peace, not bombs or body counts.

Sitting on the bed while they talk amongst each other, they offer me a
hot beverage that mimics tea with its foamy, deep brown appearance.

Each Iraqi soldier in the room takes a sip of the
foreign liquid and then passes it to me.

The glass is no taller than a shot glass; it is boiling hot in
temperature, and I almost drop it as soon as I touch it.

My answer to tasting this foreign beverage is, "No, thanks,
way too hot, you all enjoy," and I smile and give it back.

Thank God they aren't offended, and they keep grinning at me.

Still, I never feel threatened, outnumbered, or
uncomfortable around these unknown Iraqi soldiers.

Still sitting on the bed, I am told to stand up.

One tall and slender Iraqi soldier takes off his ring
and gives it to me, saying, "This is for you."

I notice that they wear their wedding rings on
the right hand instead of the left.

The reason for him taking off his ring and
giving it to me is to make me his wife!

I say, "No, thank you, I cannot accept this," and give it back to him.

He places the ring back on his finger.

Before leaving, I ask the one Iraqi soldier that could speak a

little English if he could teach me some of their language.

Although everything he says sounds like it would take me years

to even write down, I manage to convey what he is saying.

My mouth is nearly sore from repeating the words,

trying to pronounce them correctly.

The situation turns out to be something incredible!

Constantly repeating, the words become excitement

and they do not want to let me leave.

They are comfortable; so am I.

I know I have work to do.

However, when will I ever get this chance again

to be around actual Iraqi people?

Never!

Who knew I could find pleasure here?

I have to make a positive impression on these particular people,

so they can see that all Americans are not bad people!

The more I smile, the greater they feel.

Knowing that they didn't envy me makes me

feel like I am on top of the world!

Can you believe this?

I have won them over!

CNN news wouldn't believe how inspired these people would be if

we would just knock smiles into them instead of black and blue.

For a short moment, I become the United

States of America's proud example.

Symbolic of a First Lady, yet I am only human.

Shining bright as the stars on the states flag!
Take that, for they are running to me instead
of away from me, with a clear analysis!
Thanking every solider inside the room before
I leave, I am asked to take a photo.
I take nearly 102 photos with every single Iraqi soldier that is present.
Back to business.
Last thought of mine is, "Caught up in the rapture
of harmony, I knew God gave me a gift."
The smell that once made me think of a scorching street
in Baghdad's slums simply turned into a lasting effect of
something that I could adapt to, humanity and sacrifice.
Dirt became bigger than any amount of money I could ever receive.

See Yourself Out, but Come Back!

What do you think?

Did you like it?

Just like, or did you find it irresistible?

Did you feel something inside of you trigger?

Was I able to put the color in your world?

Thank you for purchasing my book; funny, because you

can't get a bootlegged book! Oh wait, yes you can!

By the way, just because this is the last page,

doesn't mean that this is over.

These messages go far beyond the aspects of

words on a page inside of a book.

The field will just change, and the date will be fresher.

This book has passion and familiarity in it,

which is how I *always* write and flow.

I am able to satisfy via words, but I am

willing to turn them into actions.

I guess you can say that you now know a little

bit more about Danielle Ann Deckard.

She takes her time to do things RIGHT.

After reading my book, I hope you can feel as I felt from the very

beginning to the very last page, and so much more after that.

Allow my words to marinate to your good heart.

I truly gave you my all in every page again.

This is the REAL thing, just part two!

From life, family, creative thoughts, personalities, differences,

love, games, grades, men, and God, you got it all and more!

Mom and Dad, I did it again, and I will continue to do it!

My stories are always just beginning.

For those of you that thought everything I did was

impossible, God bless you, too. Want an autograph?

No wait, let's just hold hands and pray instead!

The giving up was the hardest thing but I invested

time in dreaming with my eyes open!

Praise God, for this was only doable because of Him!

AuthorHouse is my dream team!

This feels so excellent; dreams are so astonishing and becoming!

Thank you for having me again and allowing me

to write my experiences to you all over the world,

while I sit on the sidelines of LIFE.

I can feel your expressions without having to see

you; feels kosher and unexplainable.

My heart has been touched just knowing that you

all support me. I tell you it's like a homecoming

of glory, and it's been my favorite by far.

Brilliant things are coming so be prepared.

Now, let's go write up a party and pop water bottles!

But wait here, my work is not done yet.